PRCL

GW00995116

WHAT'S IN THI

SELF-HARM: THE FACTS

FACT **Self-harm isn't necessarily about suicide.**
Sometimes people harm themselves because they want to die. But often it's more about staying alive. People may hurt themselves to help them get through a bad time. It's a way to cope.

FACT **People self-harm in different ways.**
Some cut their arms or legs, others bang or bruise their bodies. Self-harm also includes burning, scratching, hair-pulling, scrubbing, or anything that causes injury to the body. Some people take tablets, perhaps not a big overdose, but enough to blot things out for a while.

FACT **It doesn't mean you're off your head.**
All sorts of people self-harm. Even people in high-powered jobs. It's a sign that something is bothering and upsetting you, not that you are mad.

FACT **Lots of people self-harm.**
You may not have met anyone else who self-harms and may even think you are the only one who does it. There's a lot of secrecy about self-harm. But many thousands of people cope in this way for a while.

SELF-HARM: THE FACTS

FACT **It's not 'just attention-seeking'.**
People self-harm because they are in pain and trying to cope. They could also be trying to show that something is wrong. They need to be taken seriously.

FACT **It can happen once, or many times.**
Some people attempt suicide or hurt themselves just once or twice. Other people use self-harm to cope over a long time. They might hurt themselves quite often during a bad patch.

FACT **People do stop self-harming.**
Many people stop self-harming - when they're ready. They sort their problems out and find other ways of dealing with their feelings. It might take a long time and they might need help. But things can get better.

FACT **Other things can be 'self-harm' too.**
Things like starving, overeating, drinking too much, risk-taking, smoking and many others are also types of 'self-harm'. Some coping methods (like burying yourself in work) may be more acceptable, but can still be harmful.

2

UNDERSTANDING
YOURSELF

 Why do people self-harm? Usually because it helps them to cope or escape when they are having a really hard time.

If you often feel in such pain that you hurt yourself, there's a reason. Things which have happened to you, to make you feel so awful.

Some of these things may have happened to people who self-harm:

☹ Losing someone really important to them

☹ Not being loved, listened to and cared for enough

☹ Having too much expected of them or being put down

☹ Being raped, beaten or abused in some way

☹ Being seriously ill or disabled

☹ Being bullied, harassed, hated or discriminated against

Many other things may have caused the hurt in people's lives. These are just a few. Your personal experience is what matters.

3

It might also be practical, everyday circumstances that are causing you pain or making it more difficult to cope.

These sorts of circumstances often include:

⤷ Being homeless

⤷ Being unemployed

⤷ Having no money

⤷ Being pregnant or on your own with a baby

⤷ Going into prison

⤷ Being very isolated

"I started self-harming when I was little - just scratching and banging myself. It was because of all the rows and craziness in my family. It got worse when I left Care and I was living on my own in this horrible room, with no support and nothing to do."

If things like this (or any other painful things) have happened to you, you might think you should just 'get over it' and cheer up. But your feelings matter and need to be taken seriously. Later on we'll talk about ways of helping yourself and getting help with things.

Next we'll see why some people deal with difficult experiences like these through self-harm.

BUT WHY SELF-HARM?

Self-harm is often a way of coping with the feelings caused by things that have happened to you. It can work in different ways:

"LETTING OUT THE SCREAM INSIDE"

"Sometimes I feel like I'm going to die from all the sadness inside me. When I cut it's like my body is crying for me, letting out some of the agony."

Often people self-harm because they feel so awful inside. Their feelings hurt so much, they are unbearable. Lots of people say that their self-harm is a way of coping with the terrible pain they feel about the things that have happened to them in their lives.

When feelings are bottled up inside, they can become overwhelming. But often it's hard for people to express their feelings. Sometimes they self-harm as a way of showing their hurt and sorrow.

"It's like there's all this pain inside me, and it can't come out. When I see a wound on me it's like I'm showing how I really feel inside."

"TAKING MY MIND OFF IT ALL"

Sometimes people hurt themselves because it helps take their mind off painful feelings. It's like a distraction.

"If I've got a burn or something on my arm, it takes the focus off what I'm feeling. It hurts, but it lets me stop feeling the hurt inside me, which is worse."

When people just can't bear to think about their experiences and problems, they might self-harm to get away from it all for a while.

"Some days I wake up and it's all there inside me, and I feel so down, and I just can't face it. Then I'll take some of my Mum's pills and get out of it."

Some of the ways people can feel before they self-harm include:

Upset
Sad
Hurt
Desperate
Hopeless
Wound-up
Broken-hearted
Numb or 'dead'

You might have different ways of saying how you feel. It might be different at different times.

6

"SOMETHING I'M IN CONTROL OF"

You may feel that others are controlling what happens to you. Or maybe people have abused their power over you in the past. It can be pretty awful to feel powerless, whether it's about where you live, how people treat you, getting a job, or even what you feel. Other people may not realise how powerless you feel.

"I've always had to do what suited other people - different foster parents, children's homes, schools. Nobody ever asked me what I wanted."

Young people are often not consulted about things that affect their lives. This is wrong and can leave them feeling desperate.

Injuring yourself might help you to feel you have control over something in your life. If people have hurt you in the past (or more recently), then it might feel better that **you** are the person hurting you now.

"It's like a control thing. How deep, how often, where I cut - it's all down to me. It's my body and I'll decide what to do with it."

Taking some control in this way shows you don't want to be powerless. Perhaps you will gradually be able to take control in some of the other areas of your life.

"A TIME-BOMB TICKING INSIDE ME"

Anger is a very important emotion. It's what can fire us up to fight something we know is wrong. It can help us stick up for ourselves. But it's often hard to know what to do with angry feelings which build up inside. Sometimes self-injury is a way of getting out some anger.

"I get mad about things, it all knots up inside me and I just want to scratch myself and slash at myself."

A lot of people feel like it's not okay for them to get angry. They might have been brought up to think it's 'not nice'. Or been punished if they shouted or showed any anger.

The result of this can be that sometimes people don't even realise they're angry. Or they think things are their fault and take their anger out on themselves.

"I hit myself because I'm so angry with myself - for being so stupid and pathetic, for being the sort of person bad things happen to."

Sometimes self-harm (even if it is hidden) can feel like a way of getting back at people you're angry with. This might happen if people have hurt you and you are scared to be angry with them:

"After I cut myself I feel good, like I've punished them, secretly. I can be talking to them and I can feel my arm and it's like 'stuff you', like I've got one over on them."

"GETTING OUT THE BADNESS"

Self-injury can be a way of punishing yourself. This doesn't mean you have done something wrong. It might be that other people have done something wrong to you. But this can leave **you** feeling guilty and bad about yourself.

People sometimes hurt themselves so they can feel they have had the punishment they think they deserve. Then they don't have to feel so guilty or 'bad':

"The badness I feel becomes unbearable. I can't take it any more so I cut. The relief is instant. It's like I've got what I deserve. The badness just drains away."

Sometimes people are made to feel as though they are dirty. (This often comes from abuse or rape.)

"Washing doesn't work, however much I do it. I cut myself where I was touched. It gets rid of the dirt."

It's bad enough having been hurt by other people. Punishing yourself for it might make you feel better for a little while, but it means you end up being hurt all over again. It doesn't seem fair.

It's good if you want to get rid of some guilt and 'bad' feelings. But those who have hurt you are to blame for what you have suffered. Maybe it's time you started being angry with them, instead of yourself?

9

"AN EXCUSE FOR SOME COMFORT"

For some people self-harm is about coping with horrible feelings of emptiness inside. It can seem like nothing can fill the great, lonely space.

"When I feel empty it's like there is nothing inside me. I'd do anything to fill that gaping hole. I used to stuff myself with food but it was never enough. But when I cut it just goes."

Sometimes the emptiness is about a need for comfort. Perhaps it feels like you don't deserve comfort. Some people have never received the love and caring they need, so they don't know how to give it to themselves.

Self-harm can make it easier to give something to yourself. There's something 'real' wrong that needs taking care of.

"I like looking after my cuts. It's the one time I can be really nice to myself. Then I curl up in bed and just snuggle down and go to sleep."

Sometimes self-harm can give you a reason to go to someone else for some looking after.

"It gave me an excuse to go the nurse and be bandaged up and taken care of."

This doesn't mean you are 'just attention-seeking'. It means you have a desperate need for some real caring.

"SHOWING THERE'S SOMETHING WRONG"

Sometimes self-harm is a desperate way of trying to communicate to other people. You might be trying to send a signal that something bad is happening to you.

"I thought if I had bruises on me, someone would realise that things weren't all right at home, and would make it stop, somehow."

Or you could be trying to show that you can't cope.

"People always think I'm happy and together. Even if I say that I'm down they think it's not serious. In the end I took tablets - not to die but to prove I wasn't okay."

People sometimes self-harm if they think others won't take any notice of their feelings - that just telling them they're hurt and angry won't have enough effect.

"I wanted my Dad to feel bad, to realise that it mattered what he'd done to me. That I was screwed up by it. I wanted him to be sorry."

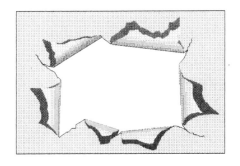

11

"SOMETHING THAT'S MINE"

Sometimes self-injury can be a way of having something of your own. You might feel like you haven't got much that's yours, that other people don't own or interfere with. There might not be people in your life who really know and stick by the real you.

"Self-harm - it's something special I do for myself, it's mine, my secret. Like a friend, just for me."

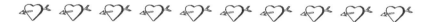

"THIS IS ME"

Self-harm might also feel like a way you try to be true to yourself. Perhaps you feel like you have to hide parts of yourself. If you can't show your feelings, or say what you think about things, hurting yourself can be a way of saying (even secretly) 'this is who I am'.

Or if you can't live the way you want to, and are expected to live up to what other people think you should be, maybe hurting yourself is a protest.

"Cutting is like part of me, my identity. Sometimes when people are having a go at me about 'looking nice' or getting a good job or something (and I'm keeping my mouth shut), I think about my arms and my scars and then I don't care."

"AN ESCAPE HATCH" - SUICIDE

Often, the reasons people kill themselves (or try to) are like the reasons people self-injure. They are in terrible emotional pain. They feel desperate. There's usually also some other things happening:

They've lost hope
The person can't face having to stay alive and keep feeling like this. They feel trapped and powerless. It seems like no-one cares or can help.

"I was really depressed, panicky all the time. I thought no-one liked me. I didn't know what was happening - I thought it was all my fault. I couldn't see any future."

They're frightened
Perhaps they are dreading something which is going to happen. Or scared of the consequences of something that they have done. Maybe they think they are going to get into trouble, or that someone is going to hurt them.

"Trying to kill myself was a lot to do with my sexuality. I thought when people found out I was gay my life wouldn't be worth living. Also I couldn't cope at school and I couldn't keep covering it up."

They want to join someone else who has died
"After my mum died, I couldn't bear going on without her. It felt so empty and pointless. Also I felt like what right did I have to go on living when she couldn't? I thought I should go and keep her company."

13

If you feel like killing yourself:

In this book we're not saying "don't self-harm". But killing yourself is different. We don't want you to die.

Sometimes knowing you **could** kill yourself, if things get really unbearable, can help you cope and carry on. But if you ever seriously feel like you want to die, try to think about these things:

REASONS NOT TO KILL YOURSELF

❖ Your feelings, awful though they truly are, won't stay the same for ever. Things can get better. You can't imagine it now, but you will have happy times again.

❖ The terrible thing about suicide is that it is final. You can't change your mind and come back.

❖ If people don't want to see how they've hurt you, they still won't. And anyway, you won't be around to enjoy seeing them upset and sorry!

❖ You matter, and you deserve the chance to have your life and to live it in your way for you.

❖ There **are** other ways out of your situation, and there are people who will help you find them (see page 27).

"Thinking back to how I felt before I took the overdose I couldn't have imagined all the good things that have happened since. I'm glad I didn't miss out on them."

14

STAYING SAFE

WHY BOTHER?

Just because you hurt yourself doesn't mean your safety and your health don't matter. It's important to keep the damage to the minimum. You deserve to take the best care of yourself you can, while you're self-harming.

DAMAGE LIMITATION

- Don't mix self-harm with alcohol or drugs or you might go further than you meant to.

- Get a tetanus jab, and a booster every 10 years.

- Use only clean things to cut, and don't share.

- Don't assume that over-the-counter drugs aren't dangerous. You can still die of a small overdose, especially of paracetamol.

- If you're really wound-up and likely to do something drastic, get yourself away from things you can hurt yourself with. Try to be with people.

NEED ADVICE?

If you are worried about your self-harm or not sure what to do, ask a pharmacist (at the chemist's) for advice, or ring Accident and Emergency or your GP.

TAKING CARE OF YOURSELF

✝ Clean cuts gently and put on a dry, clean, non-stick dressing, or use 'steristrips' to close.

✝ Cool burns with cold water. (The injury can keep getting worse even after you've stopped burning. It's worth cooling for up to half an hour.) Then put on anti-inflammatory cream or dressing.

✝ Treat yourself kindly and calmly - you've had a shock. Rest and comfort yourself.

THE DANGER ZONE

Get medical help quickly for:

☠ Cuts that are deep or wide

☠ Bleeding that spurts or won't stop

☠ Burns or scalds bigger than a 50p

☠ Infection - area red, hot, swollen or oozing pus

☠ Overdoses and poisons

SCARED TO GO TO ACCIDENT & EMERGENCY?

Take a friend or supporter. Be polite but stick up for yourself. You have the right to decent treatment. You can get more advice from the National Self-harm Network (see page 27).

THINGS TO DO FOR YOURSELF

This section is **not** just about saying *"do this instead of self-harming"*.

If you want to hurt yourself, no-one has the right to try to stop you. Self-harm might be the best way you have found to help you cope with your life at the moment. Maybe you don't even want to think about giving up self-harm.

"When people mentioned giving up I would just switch off. I thought if they didn't understand how impossible it was to stop then they didn't understand anything."

But it is possible to deal with some of the pain that makes you hurt yourself.

In the next few pages there are ideas for thinking about your life, your difficulties, and your hopes and dreams. We'll also talk about taking care of your feelings and needs.

If you find ways of dealing with painful things then you might find you don't want to self-harm as often. You can stay in control and have choices about how you cope.

THINKING ABOUT YOUR LIFE IN THE PAST

Things which have happened to you in the past still affect you now. They might be partly why you self-harm. But people can get over painful things, and there are things which can help:

- **Remembering what has happened to you**

- **Believing your memories - taking them seriously**

- **Allowing yourself feelings about the past**

- **Seeing how your experiences have affected you**

One good thing to do is to tell the story of your life. You can tell it to yourself, and to someone else if you want to. You can do it a bit at a time, or all at once - whatever helps you make sense of your life and your feelings.

"When I wrote about my life I was shocked. It was like something out of a film. But it all happened to me and I began to see there were real reasons for what I felt."

There are lots of ways of telling your story:

You could make a tape of yourself talking.

You could make a scrap book about it, with photos, letters, school reports, drawings, and bits of writing.

You could show it on a time-line, marking on the important things that have happened since you were born.

THINKING ABOUT YOUR LIFE NOW

What things in your life at the moment feel good, or okay?
What gets you down, makes you feel bad?

THINGS THAT ARE IMPORTANT TO HOW YOU FEEL INCLUDE:

- *Where you live and who with*

- *Relationships (friends, parents, boyfriends/girlfriends)*

- *Job, school, college, or what you do with your days*

- *Things you do for pleasure - like going out*

- *Money and practical things*

You could think about each of these and work out what's
good and what's bad for you in your life. For instance, you
might have some friends you feel good with. But there
might be some other people in your life who treat you
badly, who seem to make you feel horrible.

*"I realised I don't have to spend my time with tossers
who put me down. Or have sex with everyone who
shows an interest in me."*

Which things would you like to change? What do you need
to do to change these?

*"I needed to get away from everything: parents,
college which I hated, being stuck in a rut,
being seen as a nutter. I went away to a
Community Service Volunteers project. It was a good
laugh. And it really turned things round for me."*

19

THINKING ABOUT WHAT YOU WANT FOR YOURSELF

Often young people feel they don't have a chance to think about what they want or where they are going. Maybe other people have been telling them what to do all their lives. Or nobody has ever cared and they can't imagine much future. And anyway, it can seem like there aren't many opportunities around.

"I never let myself think about what I wanted. What was the point if you couldn't have it? But it meant I had nothing to try for or dream about."

Often other people seem to expect you to be like them. But it's important to be you, to have your own hopes and dreams and aims. If you're not sure what you want, a good way of finding out is to imagine yourself sometime in the future, say a few years from now. How you'd like things to be.

In your fantasy:

★ What sort of person are you?
★ Where are you?
★ What things are you doing?
★ What things are you interested in and exploring?
★ What kinds of people are important in your life?

The next thing is to think about some small ways to begin working towards just some of these things. You **can** be you and go for what you want. There's lots of time. It may not all be possible - but some of it will be.

EXPRESSING YOUR FEELINGS

If you self-harm, it's likely there are important feelings inside you which need to be honoured and expressed.

Some of the feelings that hurt so much inside might have been there a long time. They might be about things that have happened in the past, as well as now. Feelings we bury don't go away, unfortunately. They stay inside, making us feel miserable, frozen, or wound-up.

It can be hard and painful to let out your feelings. But it can also be a big relief, and make more space inside you for new, good feelings.

WAYS YOU CAN EXPRESS YOUR FEELINGS INCLUDE:

Keeping a diary - of your thoughts and feelings

Talking - to someone who'll listen

Drawing - not 'art', but shapes and colours

Writing letters - not necessarily to send

Writing poetry, stories, or just odd words

Listening to music - which fits how you feel

Crying - into your pillow if need be

A punchbag, drum, dartboard.... (improvise!)

Shouting and swearing (on paper if not aloud)

TAKING CARE OF YOURSELF

! ! ! Important ! ! ! Don't skip this bit ! ! !

Taking care of yourself - in lots of ways - is the most important thing you can do. But it's hard to let yourself. You might feel like you don't deserve it. (Not true.)

Sometimes you might think *"Why should I take care of myself? No-one else cares about me, why should I?"* Or it might seem like if you're taking care of yourself then it's like denying the pain you're still in.

Taking care of yourself doesn't mean everything's okay and you're fine on your own. You still need other people. But it is a good way of feeling a bit better, and being happier.

BELIEVING IN YOURSELF

You've probably been told lots of bad things about yourself. You need to chuck those messages out. Accept yourself - you are okay just as you are. You can turn things around by thinking about:

 good things about yourself

 reasons why you don't deserve to be put down

"When I feel like shit I try to say to myself 'you're not the bad one' and remember things like I'm a kind person, that I'm good fun sometimes, stuff like that."

TREATING YOURSELF WELL

You need to look after your body and your mind. Start with small things. These can really change how you feel.

Some important things to do for yourself:

  Make sure you get enough sleep and food.

 Find ways to relax and switch off - *like music, reading, a bath, aromatherapy, computer games...*

 Do things your body enjoys - *like dancing, gym, weights, cycling, swimming, walking...*

☺ ☺ ☺ Don't be isolated - *phone and see friends, join a support group, even get a pen-pal (SHOUT mag. can put you in touch with others who self-harm - see page 27).*

COMFORTING YOURSELF

When you feel bad, you need and deserve comfort. You would probably be good at comforting someone else who was upset (say a child). You can do the same for you.

Things that might comfort you could include:

♥ *putting yourself to bed with a hot drink*

♥ *a cuddle with your cat, pillow or teddy*

♥ *sitting under a tree or anywhere that lifts your spirit*

♥ *talking gently to yourself*

♥ *having a favourite food*

♥ *watching kids' T.V.*

♥ *getting yourself a little present*

23

GETTING HELP

If you are having a hard time, you have the right to some help with it. You deserve support. People often find it hard to go to someone else for help.

This might be because:

❖ They're scared their parents or friends will find out

❖ They think it's weak or stupid to need some help

❖ They can't see how anyone else can help them

❖ They're worried they won't be taken seriously, or the person will think they're mad, or have a go at them.

These worries and doubts are understandable. But if things are bad for you and you don't seem to be able to sort them out on your own or with your friends or family, then you really might find it useful to go to someone outside.

"I see a counsellor at a youth advice place. It's so nice that she listens to me and thinks what I say and feel is important. Usually she doesn't give advice, but she sometimes has some ideas I haven't thought of."

You can go to places where it's confidential, and no-one else will know you've been there or what you've talked about. Places where they won't think you're mad or stupid. Where it's okay if you don't know where to start. It's their job to help you talk, and to listen to you and support you.

WHERE TO TRY FOR SOME HELP

You might have to do some research to find out the best places for you, in your area. You could look in Yellow Pages, or ask at the library or Citizens' Advice Bureau. There are some places to contact for help on page 27.

Here are some possibilities:

College/school Is there a counsellor, or a pastoral or welfare adviser? What about a personal tutor?

Young people's advice centres: There's one of these in most towns. Usually you can drop in, or phone.

Helplines: Ring to talk when you're having a rough time, and to find out about other services.

Rape and abuse support services

Mental Health groups (e.g. MIND)

Your GP: Might refer you to a counsellor or psychologist if you say you need someone to talk to.

You need to go for help when it's right for you.

But don't leave it too long.

Please reach out to someone now if you are desperate, suicidal, or if your self-harm feels out of control.

HELPING A FRIEND
WHO SELF-HARMS

If you are concerned about a friend who self-harms you might be wondering how best to help. It can be hard to know what to do.

The most useful things you can offer are:

✳ Listen and find out what your friend needs

✳ Show you care but be aware of your limits

✳ See the person rather than the injuries

✳ Understand that it's about important feelings

✳ Support what they want to do

It is also important to know what **not** to do, so here are a few don'ts:

☞ Don't think you can stop them if they don't want to

☞ Don't feel responsible

☞ Don't try to make them feel guilty

☞ Don't tell other people without their consent

Remember it's just a way of coping, like others, even if you find it shocking. But if you want to be there for your friend make sure you look after yourself. Supporting someone through a hard time can be very draining.

PLACES TO CONTACT

Anti-bullying Campaign: Help about bullying. 0207 378 1446.

Bristol Crisis Service for Women: Helpline and booklets on self-injury. PO Box 654 Bristol BS99 1XH. 0117 925 1119.

Careline: Confidential counselling on any issue. Mon-Fri 10am-4pm. 0208 514 1177. Several Asian languages spoken.

Childline: For young people in trouble or danger. Freephone 0800 1111. 24 hours. Or write to Childline, Freepost 1111.

Eating Disorders Association: Information and support. Helpline 01603 621414. Youth helpline (up to 18) 01603 765050

London Lesbian and Gay Helpline: 24-hours. 0207 837 7324.

MIND Info Line: Information on all aspects of mental distress and treatment. 0345 660163. Mon-Fri 9.15am-4.45pm.

National Self-harm Network: Info and campaigning for people who self-harm. PO Box 16190 London NW1 3WW

Samaritans: Crisis support. 24 hours. 0345 909090.

Who Cares? Linkline: Information and support to young people who are or have been in Care. Freephone 0500 564 570

Women's Aid Federation: For women and children suffering domestic violence. 0117 963 3542.

Youth Access: Will put you in touch with young people's support projects in your area. 0208 772 9900.